Words That Heal
Encouragement for The Soul

Second edition

STACIE P. THOMPSON

Words the Heal: Encouragement for the Soul

Stacie P. Thompson

Published by

Love/Self Love

Foreword

It has been eight years since the first edition of Words That Heal: Encouragement for the Soul was published. As the number eight is often believed to signify new beginnings, this new work remains new today in ways that reveal a wiser, stronger, and more resilient Stacie, its author. As readers engage each heartfelt expression of enlightenment and encouragement, it is my sincere hope that time is taken to savor the seasoning of each that is ripe with the hindsight, insight, and foresight of a woman who valiantly regards her wounds and wins as fertilizer for her personal evolution and maturity. This offering has not been given to its readers from an "I know it all" perspective but rather one that says, "Join me as I teach what I learn," which makes it a delightful experience for the self-aware, lifelong learner who embraces change as an invaluable gift and for the one who desires a new lease on life.

Paulleatha Bruce, D. Min

Christian Leader and Entrepreneur

Introduction

In 2015, I took a leap of faith and shared my heart with the world through my first book, "The Words That Heal: Encouragement For The Soul." It was a profound moment in my journey as a motivational speaker and author. In those pages, I poured out my life experiences, heartfelt prayers, and the transformative journey of healing upon which I had embarked. My goal was clear: to touch the lives of others and offer them the guidance and inspiration they needed.

Since that pivotal year, life has continued to unfold in unexpected ways. I have faced new challenges, celebrated remarkable victories, and encountered countless individuals who shared their stories with me. I have grown, evolved, and gathered a wealth of wisdom and insight along the way.

In 2023, I stand at a crossroads, feeling a powerful call to action. I have reached a point where I have had enough — enough of holding back, enough of remaining silent. I have something burning inside me, a message that demands hearing. It is a message of resilience, unwavering determination, and boundless hope.

As a motivational speaker and author, my journey is far from over. I am ready to embark on a new chapter, to share my updated experiences, and to continue uplifting and inspiring people. Through my words, I aim to ignite a fire within others, to help them find their own strength, and to remind them that healing is possible, no matter how daunting the journey may seem. So, here and now, I declare my commitment to making a lasting impact, and I invite you all to join me on this exciting new adventure. Together, we will create a world filled with hope, encouragement, and the transformative power of words.

My Apologies

Stacie,

I want to express my heartfelt apologies for the times when I failed to set clear boundaries.

I deeply regret putting others before you, and I know first-hand the pain it caused.

Allowing the opinions of others to shape how I saw you was a mistake. I should have had more faith in your judgment and self-worth.

Sharing your innermost desires prematurely and with too many people was an error in judgment. I should have respected your trust and kept those dreams between us until the time was right.

Trusting too early and with the wrong people was a grave misstep, and I am sorry for any consequences it may have had.

I also apologize for giving my attention to those who did not deserve it, diverting my focus from you when it should have been solely on nurturing your relationship with God.

Feeling unloved is something I deeply regret, as I should have made you feel cherished and valued every day.

Lastly, expecting too much from others, hoping they could fulfill what only you truly deserve, was unrealistic, and I apologize for any undue pressure that was placed on you.

Stacie, I hope you can find it in your heart to forgive me for these shortcomings. My intention is to grow, heal, and learn from these mistakes so that when we speak and share with others, they witness how God turned every one of your dreams into reality.

PURPOSE

Finding Purpose

Life has a remarkable way of exposing us to heartache, loss, grief, and those challenging setbacks that sometimes feel overwhelming. But during these trials, I have discovered a powerful anchor that has kept me steady, focused, and stronger than I ever imagined – and that anchor is knowing My Purpose in life.

It is not just a vague notion; it is a burning passion, a clear direction that guides every step I take. My purpose is my North Star, my unwavering source of motivation. It pushes me each day to keep going, to rise above the obstacles that life places in my path. And let me tell you, discovering your purpose can be the most transformative journey you embark upon.

When you find your purpose, it becomes a lifeline in the storm. The force propels you forward when you want to give up. It is the reason you wake up with determination, even in the face of adversity. Your purpose is unique, a God-given calling that aligns with your passions, talents, and values. It is the driving force that gives your life profound meaning and direction.

So, I encourage you to embark on your journey of self-discovery. Seek out that purpose that ignites a fire within you. And once you find it, hold on to it with unwavering determination. Let it be the compass that guides your decisions, the motivation that keeps you going, and the source of your inner strength.

Stacie Quote... "Life may throw challenges your way, but with Purpose as your guiding light, you'll navigate through them with resilience and emerge stronger than ever before!"

Sifting

"Stop chasing what God has sifted." These words carry profound wisdom that I have come to understand through my own journey. It is expected to try to hold on to people, places, and things removed from our lives, but doing so can hinder our progress.

God's plan often involves pruning away elements from our lives that no longer serve our greater purpose. It might be painful and leave us feeling empty, but it is a necessary process. These removals are not punishments; they are redirections.

Continuing to chase and retrieve what is gone is like trying to swim against the current. It exhausts us and keeps us stuck in a cycle of longing and frustration. It prevents us from moving forward towards the new blessings and opportunities that await us.

Embracing God's sifting process means trusting in His divine plan. It means letting go of the past and having faith that what is meant for us will come at the right time. By releasing the need to cling to what is no longer in our grasp, we free ourselves to receive the abundance and fulfillment that lies ahead on our unique journey.

Stacie Quote... "Have faith and let go of what has been sifted from your life. Trust that God's plan is unfolding as it should, and as you do, you will find the freedom and peace to move forward towards the blessings that await you."

Routine or Purpose

In the realm of existence, there are two paths to tread: Routine or Purpose. A Routine Life entails repeating days, where each moment seems scripted, and you move through your daily tasks on autopilot. It is a life without questioning, where time appears to be your adversary. You have muttered, "I can do this in my sleep," indeed, it often feels like your eyes are closed to the world passing you by. On the other hand, Living on Purpose is an awakening.

Each dawn brings a specific goal, a fervent desire for personal fulfillment and the betterment of others. Every word and action are a conscious stride towards making an impact. Anticipation fills your heart as you embrace the unknown opportunities each day presents. Time is not rushed away in fear of missing a divine chance. Instead, you revel in humor and goodness within every situation, aiming to conquer every challenge.

As we stand at the end of each day, reflecting on its mix of good and bad, remember this: Life unfolds with its share of disappointments, heartbreak, setbacks, and failures. However, how you respond to these trials shapes your journey. You hold the power to decide how each day concludes and how the next one begins.

So, repeat after me... "I choose to conclude each day with abundant joy, love, and happiness, regardless of my current circumstances. I am stronger today because of the trials I faced. I confronted my greatest fears and emerged victorious.

Stacie Quote... "The mere fact that I am alive affirms my purpose. No longer shall I live each day in a monotonous order."

Embarking

I am embarking on an unwavering journey, relentlessly chasing after every opportunity that dares to cross my path! You see, I have realized that I owe it to myself, not just financially, but in terms of self-worth and personal growth. There were moments in my life when I questioned my worthiness and qualifications and hesitated to step into the spotlight of my potential.

But now, I have shattered those self-imposed limitations. I have decided that every experience, every challenge, and every success is an opportunity to validate my worthiness and capabilities. It is as if I am settling a debt with myself, repaying the countless hours of self-doubt with relentless determination. I believe that by pursuing these opportunities, I am not only achieving my dreams but also setting an example for others. I am showing them that no matter where you have been or what doubts have plagued your mind, you have the power to transform your life.

Stacie Quote... "Keep your head up, with unyielding spirit, to make a mark and embrace your own path to greatness!"

Follow Your Path

Follow the path God has created for you and watch how He will bless each step you take. This powerful message resonates deeply with my role as a motivational speaker and author. I believe each of us has a unique purpose in life, a divine path set before us.

I have experienced the incredible blessings of aligning with this higher purpose throughout my journey. When we have faith and trust in the path laid out by a higher power, we discover a profound sense of guidance and support. It is as if God conspires to help us achieve our goals and dreams.

I emphasize the importance of faith and patience when I share this message with others. Even in the face of uncertainty, knowing that we are on the right path and God is with us every step of the way can provide unwavering strength. I have seen countless individuals transformed by this belief, witnessing the blessings that unfold as they follow their unique journey.

So, remember, trust in the path laid out for you, have faith in the blessings that await, and take each step with purpose and conviction.

Stacie Quote... "The journey will not only lead you to your goals but also bring a deep sense of fulfillment and spiritual growth."

The Journey

Your journey is just as important as your destination."
This simple yet profound statement summarizes my
core message as a motivational speaker and author. It
is easy to get fixated on the end goal, the big dreams
we aspire to achieve. However, it is crucial to recognize
that every step and experience along the way is
integral to our personal growth and development.

In my own life, I have come to appreciate that it is
during the journey that we learn, evolve, and gather the
experiences and lessons that shape us. The
challenges we face, the detours we take, and the
people we meet all contribute to our story. They build
resilience, character, and wisdom.

When I stand before my audiences, I remind them that
success is not just about reaching the summit; it is
about savoring every moment of the climb. Embrace
the difficulties, for they mold you into the person
capable of reaching your destination. Cherish the

journey, for it is where you find your true self and the inspiration to keep moving forward.

Stacie Quote… "Your destination may be your goal, but your journey is where you become the person who can achieve it."

Purpose in Adversity

Your purpose is birthed through adversity, and it is something I have personally come to understand and share passionately as a motivational speaker and author. Adversity is like the vessel where our true purpose is shaped. We often discover our deepest calling in struggle, pain, and even degradation moments.

I have had my fair share of challenging experiences that could have easily broken my spirit, but my unwavering sense of purpose allowed me to stand tall. When life throws its harshest tests at us, it is easy to lose hope, but it is precisely during these trials that we can tap into our inner strength.

I have stood with my head held high in the most degrading moments in my life because I knew that my purpose was greater than any circumstance. This is a message I deliver with fervor to my audiences. I want them to realize that their purpose is a beacon of light that can guide them out of the darkest tunnels.

So, embrace adversity as the vessel that shapes your purpose, and let it be the force that empowers you to rise above life's challenges.

Stacie Quote... "Your purpose is your anchor, your source of strength, and it will lead you through the toughest storms with your head held high."

LIFE LESSONS

God's Timing

One thing I know for sure is that God's timing is faithful, true, and never too late! I have learned valuable life lessons that I never wanted to be taught when I stepped ahead of God's timetable for my life. His grace is sufficient; He is a redeemer and will restore everything you lost and more!

My advice? Be still, hear God, and when He moves you, move. It is that simple.

These words carry a profound depth of wisdom and faith. I have experienced first-hand the consequences of rushing ahead of God's plan. During those times, we often encounter the toughest challenges and setbacks.

But the beauty lies in God's unwavering grace and the promise of restoration. Even when we falter, His divine plan remains intact, ready to guide us back on course. It is a message I wholeheartedly share with my audiences, encouraging them to trust in God's timing and be attuned to His guidance.

Being still and listening to God's voice is a practice that can transform lives. It is about surrendering and following a higher purpose with unwavering faith.

Stacie Quote... 'When God moves you, indeed, move with conviction and trust that His plan is always faithful and true."

Dream Killers

Live life to the fullest every day. Do not allow anyone or anything to kill your dreams or purpose. When you find love, peace, and joy, hold on to it like your life depends on it because it does! Avoid negative people and situations, and lastly, no matter what, do what is best for you and let God take care of what others think or say.

This philosophy is the principle of the message I bring to audiences everywhere. Life is a precious gift, and it is meant to be lived with passion and purpose. I have witnessed the transformative power of embracing this mindset in my own life, and I am committed to inspiring others to do the same.

Finding and nurturing love, peace, and joy is a testament to our inner strength and resilience.

They are the guiding lights that illuminate our path. I emphasize the importance of positively surrounding ourselves and cutting ties with negativity to create a life reflecting our purpose.

As a motivational speaker and author, I urge everyone to live by these principles, for they lead to a life of fulfillment, purpose, and unwavering faith.

Stacie Quote... "The notion of doing what is best for oneself while letting go of external judgments is liberating. It is about trusting in a higher power and the unique path set before us."

Competition

The competition will hinder your progress; get the competition off your mind and focus on your goals. This is a mantra I passionately share with my audiences as a motivational speaker. I have seen countless individuals held back by the constant comparison and pressure to outdo others. But the truth is, your journey is unique, and your dreams and goals are yours alone.

When we fixate on competition, we often lose sight of our goals and potential. I have witnessed the transformative power of redirecting that energy toward one's dreams. It is about self-discovery, self-improvement, and staying true to your path. By eliminating the noise of competition, we create space for creativity, innovation, and authentic growth.

Stacie Quote... "Remember, you are not in a race against others; you are on a remarkable journey towards your dreams. Embrace the journey, cultivate your talents, and watch as your dreams become a powerful reality."

Shake It Off

"Shake It Off and Move Forward" – These words resonate deeply with me because I have walked the path of adversity, just like you have. Life has a way of blindsiding us, catching us off guard, and sometimes even manipulating our circumstances. I have been there and felt the stirg of betrayal and the weight of disappointment. But here is the powerful truth I have discovered through my journey: All Things Work Together for My Good.

It is not just a saying; it is a guiding principle. Even in the darkest of moments, when hurt, anger, or depression threatens to consume us, we must hold on to the unwavering belief that something greater is at play. For me, that something greater is my faith in God. Knowing that on the other side of my hurt is a divine blessing waiting for me, giving me the strength to shake it off and move forward.

It is not about denying our emotions but channeling them into something transformative. Every challenge we face, every setback we encounter, is an opportunity for growth and a testament to our resilience. When we shake off the negativity that seeks to hold us back, we create space for blessings, healing, and transformation to enter our lives.

Let us embrace this mantra together. Let us remember that in the face of adversity, we have the power to shake off the pain and stride confidently toward our brighter future. Life's hurdles may slow us down, but they will never stop us from reaching our full potential.

Stacie Quote... "With faith in our hearts and the determination to move forward, we can overcome anything that comes our way and emerge stronger than ever before!"

Life Challenges

Indeed, life has its moments of hardship and challenge. Through my journey, I have realized that God has a unique way of working in our lives. Every trial, every twist and turn, every mistake, hurt, disappointment, setback, heartache, and even betrayal has played a crucial role in shaping who I am today.

It is as though each experience was a piece of a grand puzzle, meticulously placed to create a masterpiece. My mistakes were valuable lessons, teaching me wisdom and resilience. The hurts I have endured have forged my empathy and compassion for others. The disappointments, setbacks, and heartaches were not roadblocks but steppingstones, propelling me towards my greater purpose.

In those moments of darkness, it may be difficult to see the bigger picture, to fathom how these trials could serve a higher purpose. But I have learned they all worked together for My Good over time. They molded me into a person who is strong, confident, and filled with unwavering faith.

My faith has become my foundation and the source of my strength. I have witnessed first-hand how God's hand was at work, even in the most challenging circumstances. And it is this knowledge that gives me the confidence to face each new day with courage and hope. I have emerged from the depths of adversity, not broken but refined and fortified.

So, remember that life's trials are part of a greater plan, no matter how difficult. They are the raw materials that, with faith and perseverance, can transform you into a resilient, confident, and faith-filled individual.

Stacie Quote... "Embrace every experience, for they are all pieces of your remarkable journey."

Her Strength

People often wonder where I find my strength, what drives me, and how I manage to keep going. Well, it all begins with the unwavering foundation of faith that resides within me. My faith is strong, like an unbreakable thread that weaves through every aspect of my life.

I passionately believe that God orders my steps. Even when life's path is uncertain or challenging, I trust in a higher purpose guiding me forward. It is this trust in divine guidance that fuels my determination.

But it is not just faith that sustains me; it is the conscious choice I make each day to embrace Love over Hate. Love is a powerful force that not only heals but also empowers. The compass directs my actions and decisions, steering me away from negativity and bitterness.

I am also fortunate to be surrounded by a network of Strong Women. Their resilience, wisdom, and support have been pillars of strength in my life. They remind me that I am never alone on this journey and can accomplish incredible things when we lift each other up.

There is no secret formula for inner strength. It comes from within, from nurturing your soul. One of the keys is to Pray more, seeking guidance and clarity in the quiet moments. In those moments of reflection, we often find the strength to overcome our challenges.

Another crucial step is to Wait for the answers. Patience can be an amazing ally. Sometimes, we need to let life unfold and trust that the right answers will come in time.

And finally, building a Dream Team of people who Love, Support, and Trust you are invaluable. Surrounding yourself with individuals who believe in your potential and encourage your growth is like having a team of champions in your corner.

So, my friends, remember that your strength is an incredible force that lies within you. Nurture it through faith, choose love, seek guidance, be patient, and build a support network of kindred spirits.

Stacie Quote... "You can overcome any obstacle that life places in your path and achieve greatness beyond your wildest dreams."

SELF-LOVE

Self-Love Defined

Self-love, in its truest essence, is not just a trendy phrase but a fundamental quality that should be at the core of your being. It encompasses setting boundaries, prioritizing, cherishing, and recognizing your worth.

My journey has given me first-hand insight into the profound impact of lacking self-love.

Setting boundaries is an act of self-preservation. It is understanding that your needs, your emotional well-being, and your time are valuable.

By setting clear limits, you shield yourself from being drained by excessive demands and expectations from others. This practice empowers you to honor your own needs without guilt. Putting yourself first does not equate to selfishness; rather, it is an act of self-preservation. It is akin to putting on your oxygen mask before assisting others on an airplane – you must be well to effectively help others. Prioritizing your well-being ensures you have the energy and emotional capacity to support those around you. Love is not only something you give to others; it is something you must give to yourself.

Loving yourself is acknowledging your worthiness of love, kindness, and care. Treating yourself with the same tenderness and compassion you offer to loved ones. Respecting yourself means upholding your values, principles, and self-esteem. It involves not compromising what you hold dear, even when faced with challenges or peer pressure. It is a commitment to staying true to who you are. Valuing yourself is recognizing that you are unique and irreplaceable. Your experiences, perspectives, and presence have intrinsic worth. This acknowledgment empowers you to make choices that align with your sense of self-worth. My personal journey serves as a testament to the transformative power of self-love. I have witnessed the consequences of neglecting self-love, which often leads to feelings of emptiness, burnout, and a lack of fulfillment.

Without self-love, building meaningful relationships, pursuing your dreams, or finding contentment in life becomes challenging. In conclusion, self-love is not a superficial concept but the foundation for a fulfilling and balanced life. It is the practice of setting boundaries, prioritizing, loving, respecting, and valuing yourself. Embracing self-love is an investment in your well-being and a prerequisite for living a meaningful life.

Stacie Quote... "Embrace the incredible power of self-love and always remember, never settle for anyone who does not appreciate you."

I Choose Me

"I choose me" is a declaration of self-worth, a proclamation of self-care, and a tribute to the uniqueness that defines who I am. When I utter those words, "I choose me," it is not an act of selfishness or disrespect towards anyone else. Instead, it is a commitment to nurture myself so that I can, in turn, be a source of help and support to others. Within this statement lies the recognition that my feelings matter, my dreams matter, and my identity matters. Choosing me is an act of honoring my emotions, my aspirations, my choices, and my individuality.

"I choose me" is not about mistreating or causing harm to others. It is about safeguarding my peace, my mind, and my heart. It is a testament to my self-worth and a declaration that I am indeed worth it. "It's Okay to Just Be Me!" This daily affirmation reminds us that we are special, unique, and precisely what God intended us to be. We are smart, kind, caring, honest, and beautiful in our own way. Regardless of what others may think or say about us, what God says truly matters. We are His creation, carefully designed with unique qualities.

God loves His creation, and so should we. We often ask, "Why am I this way?" Why am I tall, short, light-skinned, dark-skinned, and so forth? The answer is simple: the world needs our diversity. It would be dull if we were all the same. Our style, our uniqueness, our appearance, and our personalities contribute to the richness of life. And then there is the question, "When am I going to fit in?" The truth is, we do not need to fit in everywhere. We fit in where it truly matters – with our loved ones, faith, friends, and most importantly, God. We are not meant to be carbon copies of everyone else. We deserve the best in life, including the best friends, career, and love. Believe it, own it, and declare it daily.

Stacie Quote... "You are the best, and you deserve the best!"

Know Your Worth

Never, under any circumstance, should you allow anyone to belittle or downplay your experiences. Every tear you have shed, every hurt you have felt, and every situation you have encountered is profoundly important because they are a part of your unique journey.

In this world, it is crucial to surround yourself with people who genuinely Love, Support, and Encourage You. These individuals see your worth and understand that your experiences have shaped you into the incredible person you are today. They are the ones who stand by your side, offering a shoulder to lean on during challenging times and celebrating your victories with you.

You build a protective shield around your self-esteem and well-being by creating a circle of uplifting and supportive individuals. Their love and encouragement become a powerful force that bolsters your confidence and helps you navigate life's challenges.

Remember, you are not defined by the opinions of those who would belittle or dismiss your experiences. You are defined by your strength, resilience, and the love and support you receive from those who genuinely care about you. Never compromise on the quality of the people you surround yourself with, and always hold your experiences in the highest regard, for they are the threads that weave the tapestry of your extraordinary life.

Stacie Quote… "Against all odds, I stood in faith. In my journey as a motivational speaker and author, I have faced countless challenges, but I have always believed in the power of faith to carry me through. Life may throw its curveballs, but it is in those moments of adversity that we discover our true strength."

NOTES FROM MY HEART
STACIE P. SPEAKS

When I gave you my heart, she was Whole, Happy, and at peace. Filled with Joy and ready to Love and be Loved.

You told me you would not mistreat my heart. You listened to her pour out how she had been hurt and abused in the past.

You listened to my heart share what she had endured from others and promised you were different.

You told my heart she was safe with you and finally found where she belonged.

You sang the songs she desired to hear.

You spoke the words she yearned for
You pulled her strings and tightened your grip to give her a false sense of security.

Your lies, deceit, and flowery words alerted my heart and she watched you.

She watched your actions... how nothing you said reflected how you moved.

My heart noticed that all you had was talk, no genuine desire to love and protect, only words that sounded big and deflected.
She noticed your obvious lack of confidence, your lack of respect, love, and compassion.

You did not know that every experience from the past made my heart Stronger, Wiser, and more Confident.
When your actions caused a state of confusion, she became wise to your tricks and schemes.

If the plan were to drop my heart and leave her in a state of despair and chasing after you... IT FAILED!
The damage you inflicted felt all too familiar. She took what was meant to hurt and destroy and turned it into healing and joy for herself and others.

What You Stole from Me

You stole the opportunity for me to experience being
Loved as a wife.

You stole the opportunity for me to experience making
love and bonding with my husband.

You stole the opportunity for me to say that I have only
been married once.

You momentarily stole my peace, my joy.

What you could not steal

My Faith in God
My Trust in God
My Confidence
My Strength
My Resilience
My Happiness
My desire to Love.
My desire to be Loved.
My desire to be a Wife.

You could not steal these things because God protected and covered me in these areas. He knew I would need them to Recover, Rebuild, and Rediscover Me.

Yeah, I am hurt, angry, and mad as hell that I allowed myself to get caught up in your miserable dysfunction.

You have taught me tremendously. I have learned from familiar lessons that I now realize had to be repeated, but I got it now! I have learned from lessons I never wanted to be taught by anyone.

I have made up my mind to live on, and amid it all, I have decided to take the path towards being better and not bitter. I have given up on you and us, but not on me!

Repurposing The Pain

The year is 2018:

I lived the Happy, Healthy, Free life I had spent years building.

I was at Peace, Confident, Courageous, and Bold. It took me a while to build my happy life, and I no longer had the "empty void" feeling I had felt for years.

In that very year, I lost two of the most significant individuals in my life. These two ladies taught me to Live and enjoy life. Experiencing their deaths caused me to be devastated, lost, confused, and vulnerable.

I remember crying in my living room, asking God to fill the void again.

I received a Facebook inbox message from someone I had known for 13 years. I had not communicated with him in eight years and was incredibly surprised to see a message from him.

The message read: "I was fasting and praying for a wife, and God showed me you."

My first thoughts were.

He prayed for me! He sought God, and God revealed me to him! OMG! It is happening. It is finally happening!

Someone sees me! Sees my worth! Values me! Loves me!

Sees me as a wife! God sent him to fill the void!

That is what I had been waiting to hear! That was my prayer. I had prayed daily for years.

Every secret prayer and declaration that only God and I knew about was coming to life!

I was in a vulnerable state of mind. I had just lost two of the closest people in my life. I could not focus and did not care to think twice about how he approached me or if God really sent him.

It all looked, sounded, and felt like it was a blessing from God.

He promised to protect, provide for, respect, and honor me.

I was getting married and ready to fulfill my dream of being a wife.

The wedding was May 25, 2019, on May 30, 2019, my journal entry was:

"God, please help me! I do not know what to do! This man shows absolutely no affection towards me! It is as if I repel him. He acts as if I am repulsive to him. No physical attraction was shown towards me.

None whatsoever! What have I done? What have I done, Lord? Please help me! Please, Lord, what is going on?

I spent 14 months in a marriage being what I promised: a Faithful, Honest, Loving wife. When I say "spent," it means I gave 14 months of my life, love, time, encouragement, and motivation to someone who treated me like a roommate.

For eleven of those 14 months, my daily routine was asking God these questions:

What is wrong with me? (my hair, my weight, do I have hygiene issues) What did I do to deserve this? What do I need to change about me? Why me? How did I miss the signs?

God's response to me was consistent: Romans 8:28

He said to me, "All things work together for your good. It may not seem like any good can come out of this, but you will understand soon."

I quickly realized that what I wanted and desired did not want me.

One of the most degrading and humiliating feelings is to be rejected by the person who pursued you.

I thought I was not enough. That was the consuming thought that overwhelmed me daily. I was trying so hard to be enough. I changed who I was and put my dreams, goals, and aspirations on hold.

I purchased different clothes and accessories, became self-conscious, and even purchased various hygiene products, thinking I was the problem...because something had to be wrong with me.

Nothing worked, nothing I did, no matter what or how I changed.

Stacie was never enough for him.

My healing journey taught me that you will never be enough for someone who cannot handle all of you.

I Repurposed the pain from that humiliating experience. If I can do it with what I endured, you can too.

As I conclude my story, let me impart this wisdom...

Start by making sure you have 20/20 vision. I am not talking about going to Lens Crafters for an eye exam. What I mean is to make sure your vision is clear and that you are not looking at life through hurt eyes.

When I say looking with hurt eyes, you cannot see everyone as your enemy. Every person is not just like the person who hurt you. Everyone is not the same.

Do not internalize the pain and spew it out on anyone who comes near you. You must let it go!

Recognize people for who they are… I live by a quote from one of my favorite people, Dr. Maya Angelou. She said, "When someone shows you who they are, believe them the first time."

Sadly, I used to think the total opposite of this quote. I would try to change people into who I wanted them to be no matter what they showed me. I was the ultimate people-pleaser.

Do not allow painful, traumatic experiences to cause you to be jealous of someone else's life.

Honey, you do not know what people are going through in life. Do not envy what you see on social media or in public because no one knew I had any issues until I told them.

Put in the work, get help, and heal! Please know that healing does not look the same for everyone. You can always repurpose things that have been damaged or broken.

You can repurpose your broken heart, damaged emotions, and a damaged state of mind, but you must fix it first.

Never display or present damaged goods, including your heart, emotions, or mental state, to anyone.

Purpose is often born through pain. Operating in purpose does not come easy; we never know the full extent of the purpose God has designed for our lives, and I do not believe we have only one purpose to fulfill in life.

He has already aligned every step we will take in life.

The problem is we often make mistakes. My entire life was turned upside down through this experience! I had to make choices I never thought I would have to make.

I uprooted myself from where I lived for 8 years and moved into a 1-bedroom apartment.

I was on a mission to regain peace and would not stop until I found it again.

I had to shift my focus and stop worrying about what people say or think about me because that is none of my business anyway!

I finally figured out who I needed to fill the void I mentioned earlier and found that person. I finally found myself! And baby, I love her!

She is Fierce! She is Confident! She is Bold!

There is nothing nobody can do or say to change my mind about me!!!!

The second edition of my book, born from my life experiences, is meant to be a beacon of hope. I truly hope you were able to discover not only insight and wisdom but also "Words That Heal."

A Thank You to All My Contributors

Vanessa Earle

Calrinda Mayes

Bettye Jones

Trelithia Harbin

Lisa Russey

Myren Reynolds I

Damion Smith

Clintoria Session

Vanessa Woods

Tabitha Wright

Paulleatha Bruce

Cameron Blassingame

Shamica Benson

Barbara Sims

Danielle Holloway

Juan Richardson

Tamika Earle

About the Author

Stacie Thompson, a Published Author of "The Words That Heal: Encouragement for The Soul," is an Empowerment Speaker, Certified Professional Life Coach, Certified Parent Coach, and Mentor. With over 25 years of success in her field, Stacie is an expert in empowering individuals to embrace their purpose and turn their dreams into reality.

She holds an associate degree in criminal justice from Tri-County Technical College, a bachelor's degree in psychology from Southern Wesleyan University, and a Master of Science in Youth Development Leadership from Clemson University.

Stacie's journey is a testament to the power of strength, endurance, and direction in achieving success. As a successful professional, she leads by example, demonstrating that the decisions we make today profoundly impact our tomorrow. With her insightful guidance and unwavering dedication, Stacie inspires others to unlock their potential and discover the path to personal fulfillment.

Connect with Me

www.staciepspeaks.com